The Case for Mixed-Age Grouping in Early Education

Lilian G. Katz, Demetra Evangelou, and Jeanette Allison Hartman

National Association for the Education
of Young Children
Washington, D.C.

PHOTO CREDITS: *Cover, left row top to bottom*/Marilyn Nolt, Strix Pix, Strix Pix; *center*/Royce C. Harris; *right row top to bottom*/© Michael Tony Topix, Marietta Lynch; *p. vi*/Cleo Freelance Photo; *pp. ix, 43*/Robert J. Bennett; *p. xii*/© Bm Porter 1990—Don Franklin; *pp. 3, 22, 48*/Francis Wardle; *p. 6*/Elisabeth Nichols; *p. 8*/David Phillips; *pp. 12, 17, 40*/Nancy P. Alexander; *p. 15*/Blakely Fetridge Bundy; *p. 20*/© Crystal Images 1990; *p. 25*/Esther Mugar; *p. 28*/© 1990 Brian Veditz; *p. 31*/Hildegard Adler; *p. 34*/Lillis Larson-Kent; *p. 38*/© Michael Tony Topix; *p. 46*/Cheryl Namkung.

Second printing 1991. Third printing 1993.

National Association for the Education of Young Children
1509 16th St., NW
Washington, DC 20036–1426

The National Association for the Education of Young Children (NAEYC) attempts through its publications program to provide a forum for discussion of major issues and ideas in our field. We hope to provoke thought and promote professional growth. The views expressed or implied are not necessarily those of the Association. NAEYC wishes to thank the authors, who donated much time and effort to develop this book as a contribution to our profession.

The writing of this publication was partially supported by funds from the Office of Educational Research and Improvement (OERI), U.S. Department of Education. Opinions expressed in this report do not necessarily reflect the position or policies of OERI.

LIBRARY OF CONGRESS CATALOG CARD NUMBER: 90–061182
ISBN: 0–93598931–5
NAEYC #333

DESIGN AND PRODUCTION: Jack Zibulsky
COPYEDITING: Chris Jones and Ellyn Kestnbaum

PRINTED IN THE UNITED STATES OF AMERICA

Contents

Executive Summary v

Introduction vii

*Chapter 1/*What Is Mixed-Age Grouping? 1

*Chapter 2/*Social Effects of Mixed-Age Grouping 9

*Chapter 3/*Cognitive Basis for Mixed-Age Grouping 23

*Chapter 4/*Strategies for Mixed-Age Learning: Peer Tutoring and Cooperative Learning 29

*Chapter 5/*Mixed-Age Settings: Some Successful Examples 35

*Chapter 6/*Questions About Implementing Mixed-Age Grouping 41

Conclusion and Recommendations 49

References 51

Appendix: Suggestions for Teachers Implementing Mixed-Age Grouping 55

Information About NAEYC 60

Executive Summary

MIXED-AGE GROUPING OF YOUNG CHILDREN IN SCHOOLS AND CHILD CARE CENTERS IS EXPLORED AND ADVOCATED IN THIS BOOK. ALthough it is not a new idea in education, the practice of teaching young children of varying ages together runs counter to the typical pattern of education in the United States, which separates children into single-age classes. Mixed-age grouping is supported here for the following reasons:

1. Mixed-age grouping resembles family and neighborhood groupings, which throughout human history have informally provided much of children's socialization and education. Many young children now spend relatively little time in either family or neighborhood settings and consequently are deprived of the kind of learning made possible by interage contact.

2. Research, although incomplete, indicates that social development can be enhanced by experiences available in mixed-age grouping. Leadership and prosocial behaviors have been observed to increase.

3. Current concepts of cognitive development—the "zone of proximal development" and "cognitive conflict"—imply that children whose knowledge or abilities are similar but not identical stimulate each other's thinking and cognitive growth.

4. Research on peer tutoring and cooperative learning indicates that interaction between less able and more able children ("novices" and "experts") benefits all individuals both academically and socially.

5. Mixed-age grouping relaxes the rigid, lock-step curriculum with its age-graded expectations, which are inappropriate for a large proportion of children. Furthermore, mixed-age grouping might also lead to a reduction of screening and standardized testing in the early years.

6. Mixed-age grouping has been used successfully with young children in the United States and abroad (e.g., Britain and Sweden).

Introduction

Four-year-old Ryan is constructing a spaceship from heavy cardboard. He puts paper clips through holes to serve as control buttons and becomes frustrated and upset when they repeatedly fall out. When he requests the teacher's help, she asks him to wait. He expresses impatience, and the teacher asks five-and-a-half-year-old Rachel to help him. Ryan gladly accepts her offer to help. A few minutes later Ryan is ready to lift off.

Elisa, age three, still cries when her mother leaves her at the child care center in the morning even though it has been three weeks since she joined the group. Elisa still spends most of her time close by the teacher. Christine, age five, went through a similar stage last year. Although Christine often has a difficult time sharing things, she is emotionally very sympathetic. She is also very verbal. She expresses comfort and reassurance to Elisa and offers to be her friend and to show her how to make the magnets move. Though hesitant at first, Elisa responds to the teacher's encouragement and decides to trust Christine.

A group of four- and five-year-olds greets the arrival of new manipulative materials with great interest. Included are plastic chain links: squares, triangles, circles, pyramids, ovals. The older children begin linking pieces together, stretching the linked units from one end of the room to the other. They soon move on to counting how many of each shape are in the chain. Next, they start taking actual measurements of its length. The younger children continue joining various pieces together. During subsequent days, as the older children move on to labeling different shapes and cataloging them, the younger ones begin counting, measuring, and keeping records of their findings, just as they had seen their older classmates do earlier in the week.

F ROM WHAT WE CAN OBSERVE, CHILDREN IN ALL CULTURES LEARN FROM ONE ANOTHER. IN FAMILIES, VILLAGES, SETTLEMENTS, NEIGH-borhoods, and even transient settings such as during travel, children imitate, instruct, direct, follow, interrogate, and respond to one another's knowledge, ideas, and feelings (Whiting, 1973; Pratt, 1983; Whiting & Edwards, 1988).

> *Although humans are not usually born
> in litters, we seem to insist that they be
> educated in them.*

Pratt (1983) points out that the age-stratified culture in which we live is largely a product of the past 200 years. He suggests that "it is the result of many factors, including the size of communities, the specialization of work, the development of transportation, and the evolution of schools" (p. 7).

Around the turn of the century, when children in the industrialized nations began going to school *en masse,* a more or less uniform age of school entry was established, and progress through the grades on the basis of age became a regular practice (Pratt, 1983). Angus, Mirel, and Vinovskis (1988) point out that age-grading was part of "efficiency-oriented practices [such] as child accounting, intelligence testing, ability grouping and tracking" (p. 232).

Interest in the potential benefits of mixed-age grouping was aroused by the publication in 1959 of Goodlad and Anderson's *The Non-Graded Elementary School.* They argued that grouping children homogeneously on the basis of a single criterion (like age) does not reliably produce a group that is homogeneous on other criteria relevant to teaching and learning. Extensive research on the nongraded school movement stimulated by Goodlad and Anderson's ideas revealed, however, that its implementation consisted of "little more than ability grouping within existing grade levels" (Pratt, 1983, p. 17), and that in fact few schools actually practiced mixed-age grouping for instruction.

Curiously, though, while other settings allow children of diverse ages to interact, schools (and now child care centers) almost invariably confine interaction within a narrow age range. We place "the sixes" in first grade and, even more restrictively, we frequently divide the toddlers into "the old twos" and "the young twos." Although humans are not usually born in litters, we seem to insist that they be educated in them. To a large extent the organization of our schools seems to be based on a factory model, which uses an assembly line to subject homogeneous materials to identical treatments in order to yield uniform products.

Furthermore, schools and child care centers, particularly for preschoolers, are increasingly replacing families and neighborhoods as contexts for child-child interaction. Smaller family size and out-of-home employment for both parents lead to children spending most of their waking hours in schools and centers

Extensive research on the nongraded school movement stimulated by Goodlad and Anderson's ideas revealed that its implementation consisted of "little more than ability grouping within existing grade levels," and that in fact few schools actually practicing mixed-age grouping for instruction.

> *Multi-age grouping in the primary schools probably offers advantages over age-graded grouping for both academic achievement and social development outcomes.*

(Katz, 1988). Hence, many children have little access to other-age children.

Does this matter? Are children losing something valuable by having limited opportunity to interact with older and younger children? Are young children being especially or unnecessarily restricted by current age-grouping practices? How can these questions be answered? In this book we propose that age grouping matters in several ways. We base our case for incorporating mixed-age grouping into schools and child care centers on the accumulated experience of many early childhood educators and on research indicating its potential social and intellectual benefits. We include references to empirical studies of cross-age interaction and other related research.

A few indications of renewed interest in this topic have appeared in recent educational and developmental literature. In 1987, Goodlad and Anderson's book was reissued. In addition, the Royal Commission on Education in Canada recommended "legislation and policy changes to enable schools and school districts to establish ungraded primary divisions" (1989, p. 28).

The 1988 Task Force report of the National Association of State Boards of Education (NASBE) recommended that "early childhood units be established in elementary schools, to provide a new pedagogy for working with children ages 4–8" (1988, p. vii). Recent research on children's intellectual and social development discussed in the chapters that follow reflects increasing attention to the nature and consequences of cross-age interaction. This renewed interest in the educative potential of mixed-age grouping is welcome on both empirical and philosophical grounds.

Table 1 shows Pratt's summary of the results of 27 empirical studies reported between 1948 and 1981 that looked at the academic and social outcomes of mixed-age grouping. On balance, the table suggests that multi-age grouping in the primary schools offers advantages over age-graded grouping for both academic achievement and social development outcomes. It is our strong hunch that those benefits are likely to be even greater for younger children (e.g., children four to six years old) than for older elemen-

> *It is our strong hunch that those benefits are likely to be even greater for younger children (e.g., children four to six years old) than for older elementary-age children.*

tary-age children. However, realization of these benefits for any age range depends to some extent on both the curriculum and teaching strategies employed.

Table 1. Empirical Studies in Multi-age Grouping: 27 Studies*

	Academic Achievement	Social Development
Studies favoring conventional grouping	3	0
Inconclusive studies	12	6
Studies favoring multi-age grouping	10	9

* Based on Pratt, 1983, p. 18. Pratt does not indicate the criteria used to determine the inclusion or exclusion of the studies synthesized. The frequencies shown in Table 1 do not equal 27 because some studies had results in both columns and some did not.

In this book, we first define mixed-age grouping and examine some limitations of single-age grouping. Then, we review research on social and cognitive aspects of mixed-age grouping and describe successful multi-age programs, effective teaching strategies, peer tutoring, and cooperative learning. Finally, we present recommendations for decision makers in schools and centers for young children. An appendix contains implementation suggestions for teachers.

Chapter 1

What Is Mixed-Age Grouping?

IXED-AGE GROUPING IS PLACING CHILDREN WHO ARE AT LEAST A YEAR APART IN AGE INTO THE SAME CLASSROOM GROUPS. OVER THE years, it has been used in different ways in early childhood and primary school classes (Stahl, Stahl, & Henk, undated). Montessori classes, for instance, have traditionally been made up of children of different ages. Montessori's rationale was that younger children could learn much from the models provided to them by older children. British infant schools during the so-called Plowden years of the 1960s and 1970s taught five-, six-, and seven-year-olds in the same classes.* Mixed-age grouping has also been common in small rural schools, and cross-age tutoring has been used, in one way or another, for hundreds of years (Zindell, undated).

In recent times, mixed-age grouping has had various names: heterogeneous grouping, multi-age grouping, vertical grouping, family grouping, and primary school ungraded or nongraded classes. It should be noted that there is a distinction between the rationale for nongraded schools and for mixed-age grouping: The former is primarily intended to homogenize groups for instruction by ability or developmental level rather than by age; the latter is intended to optimize what can be learned when children of different — as well as the same — ages and abilities have opportunities to interact. Although cross-age tutoring is not identical with mixed-age classroom learning, it too takes advantage of the different competences of children of different abilities or ages as they work in pairs.

---

* No systematic research has been done on family grouping as practiced in British infant schools.

Resemblance to family and spontaneous grouping

Family units typically include heterogeneity in age. The family group provides its younger members with opportunity to observe, emulate, and imitate a wide range of competencies in all domains. Older family members have the opportunity to offer leadership and tutoring and to assume responsibility for less mature and less knowledgeable members.

Similarly, it is assumed that the wider the range of competencies in a mixed-age group, the greater will be the participants' opportunities to develop relationships and friendships with others who match, complement, or supplement their own needs and styles. The greater diversity of maturity and competence present in a mixed-age group, compared to that in a same-age group, provides a sufficient number of models to allow most participants to identify models from whom they can learn — some of whom will be of the same age, of course. However, for instructional grouping there is probably an *optimum* rather than maximum desirable diversity.

Ellis, Rogoff, and Cromer (1981) observed the composition of children's spontaneous groups in an urban setting with a population large enough to allow homogeneous age groups to form spontaneously. They reported that for all age groups strict age segregation was less common than would have been expected on the basis of common-sense notions of children's preferences. The target children were with same-age peers in only 6% of the observations, with child companions who differed in age by at least one year in 55% of the observations, and with adult companions in 28% of the observations. In this study, more often than not, children spontaneously gravitated toward heterogeneous age grouping.

Disadvantage of single-age grouping: Normative pressures

To a very large extent, current concern with developmental versus chronological age in kindergarten and first grade placement stems from the widespread use of a formal academic curriculum in these classes. Academic approaches can be thought of as homogeneous treatments that yield homogeneous outcomes only if the population it treats is homogeneous in all relevant aspects.

Our view is that mixed-age grouping in classes that employ an informal intellectually oriented curriculum can minimize the pitfalls of both kinds of segregation: by age and by readiness.

> *Some administrators report that, in mixed-age grouping, teachers' tendencies to teach all children the same lessons at the same time are reduced.*

If children spontaneously form heterogeneous peer groups, why do adults typically segregate them by age? One reason might be that, as impressions we have gained from our own experience suggest, when children in a class are close in age, teachers and parents tend to expect them to be ready to learn the same things at the same time. Indeed, from a normative point of view, such an expectation is reasonable, but the effect can be to penalize children who don't happen to meet these expectations.

Such normative pressures are currently associated with extensive screening and testing before and after the kindergarten year. The purpose of these tests is to assign to special "developmental" or "transitional" classes children deemed unready to succeed in an academic curriculum (Graue & Shepard, 1989). Or, following the notion of "a gift of a year" (Gesell Institute of Human Development, 1982), age-eligible children are withheld from school entrance on the basis of their so-called developmental age. The Gesell Institute advocates developmental rather than chronological age as a criterion of readiness to begin formal schooling, thus acknowledging the insufficiency of age as a criterion for grade placement. The practice of withholding children from school for a year is expected to result in greater homogeneity of *developmental* age in classes even though it produces a wider *chronological* age spread in the withheld children's subsequent primary classes. We agree that chronological age *per se* is an insufficient criterion of readiness for academic instruction. Our view, however, is that mixed-age grouping in classes that employ an informal intellectually oriented curriculum can minimize the pitfalls of both kinds of segregation: by age and by readiness.

When classes are mixed so that the children range in age from four to six, for example, a wider range of behavior is likely to be accepted and tolerated than in a same-age group. Furthermore, in mixed-age classes, it may be easier for kindergarten and preschool teachers to resist the "push down" phenomenon — the trend to introduce the primary school curriculum into kindergarten and preschool classes (Connell, 1987; Gallagher & Coche, 1987). Some administrators report (to the first author) that, in mixed-age grouping, teachers' tendencies to teach all children the same lessons at the same time are reduced. Mixed-age grouping compels

> *In a multidimensional class in which children have some real choice about what work they do and when or how to do it, they are more likely to make ego-enhancing choices that lead to positive self-evaluations.*

educators to organize learning activities and the curriculum so that individuals and small groups of children can undertake different kinds of work along side one another, and so that individuals can make different contributions to the group's efforts. Moreover, because mixed-age grouping invites cooperation and other forms of prosocial behavior and appears to minimize competitive pressures on children, discipline problems that seem inherent in competitive environments are often substantially reduced. The cooperation that can flourish in a mixed-age group can generate a class ethos marked by caring rather than competitiveness; the classroom culture is more likely to be characterized by helpfulness and magnanimity on the part of those able and expected to assist those who are less able. This is not to suggest that cooperation, other forms of prosocial behavior, and a caring ambience cannot be fostered in same-age classrooms, of course. Indeed, it is difficult to understand why a cooperative community atmosphere is not more common in early childhood classrooms.

Mixed-age classes are multidimensional

Rosenholtz and Simpson (1984) highlight the contrast between single and mixed grouping with their description of uni- and multidimensional classrooms. A unidimensional classroom defines academic ability and work narrowly and uses a restricted range of performance criteria to evaluate children. In these classes, the assigned tasks tap only a limited range of children's abilities and interests. On the other hand, multidimensional classes, whether single-age or mixed, offer a comparatively wide range of activities in which varying levels of skills can be applied. A variety of performance criteria are valued and accepted as legitimate. In the unidimensional classroom, the "absence of alternative definitions of what constitutes valued work prevents each student from choosing the definition that most enhances the self" (Rosenholtz

Cooperation, other forms of prosocial behavior, and a caring ambience can also be fostered in same-age classrooms, of course. Indeed, it is difficult to understand why a cooperative community atmosphere is not more common in early childhood classrooms.

> *The mixture of ages may increase
> teachers' awareness of developmental
> discrepancies within a particular child.*

& Simpson, 1984, p. 22). Therefore, a larger number of children is "forced to accept low self-evaluations" (p. 22) than would be the case in multidimensional classes. In a multidimensional class in which children have some real choice about what work they do and when or how to do it, they are more likely to make ego-enhancing choices that lead to positive self-evaluations (Greenberg, 1990). Categorizing classes as uni- or multidimensional is not simply dichotomous; probably many degrees of dimensionality exist. However, when *early childhood* classes are composed of a single-age group, the likelihood is great that its purpose is to narrow the range of learning activities and performance requirements, based on the faulty assumption that children of the same age learn the same things at the same time in the same way.

Mixed-age groups allow for children's uneven development

Most young children are not equally mature in all domains of development at a given time. For example, a child might be considerably more able in verbal reasoning but less socially adept than her age-mates. The mixture of ages may increase teachers' awareness of developmental discrepancies within a particular child. The manifestations of uneven developmental levels may also be more acceptable to teachers and caregivers in mixed- and in single-age groups. As already suggested, a wider range of behavior is likely to be accepted in a mixed-age than in a same-age group.

A mixture of ages within a class can be particularly desirable for children functioning below age-group norms in some areas of their development. These children may find it less stressful to interact with younger peers in areas in which they lag behind their age-mates. Such interactions with younger peers can enhance children's motivation and self-confidence (Kim, 1990).

Chapter 2

Social Effects of Mixed-Age Grouping

ONE OF THE MANY REASONS FOR BRINGING GROUPS OF CHILDREN TOGETHER IN THE EARLY YEARS IS TO FACILITATE AND ENHANCE THEIR social development. Indeed, the serious long-term consequences of early social difficulties demonstrated by recent research suggest that the first of the "4 Rs" in education should stand for *relationships,* particularly peer relationships (Asher & Parker, in press; Mize & Ladd, in press).

This chapter examines social development as seen in children's interactions in mixed-age groups. A majority of studies reported here use experimental methods in which children interact in mixed- or single-age groups, and comparisons are made between the quality of the interaction in the two conditions. Most of the studies were conducted in classrooms or similar environments where children spent substantial amounts of their time. The studies reviewed focus on *(1)* how children perceive one another and adapt their behavior and expectations accordingly, *(2)* how children exhibit specific prosocial behaviors in mixed-age situations, and *(3)* how children's group participation varies.

Social perceptions

Social perceptions are related to the function and purpose of the group and to the roles that individuals hold within it. In mixed-age groups, the diversity of social perceptions can support a cooperative climate. When French (1984) asked groups of first and third graders to assign various role labels to photographs of same-age,

> *In mixed-age groups, older children are perceived as contributing, and younger children as needing their contributions.*

younger, and older peers, she found both older and younger children associated specific expectations with each age group. Younger children assigned instructive, leadership, helpful, and sympathizing roles to older children. In return, older children perceived younger ones as requiring more help and instruction. Age seemed to be a significant perceptual cue in interpreting the appropriateness of role behavior in a given context.

In mixed-age groups, then, older children are perceived as contributing, and younger children as needing their contributions. These mutually reinforcing perceptions thus create a climate of expected cooperation beneficial to children, and to teachers who often can feel that they (as the older ones) must do all the giving.

Interestingly, in French's study, age was not an important factor in friendship choice, indicating that mixed-age grouping does not necessarily limit children's friendships. In fact, friendship appears to be a relationship that transcends age-related behavior. Brody, Stoneman, and MacKinnon (1982) investigated interaction among school-age children. They evaluated patterns of behavior among younger siblings, their friends, and school-age peers according to the quality of the interactions. They observed the various roles children assumed in different combinations of dyads and triads while playing a game. The assumed roles were teacher, learner, manager, managee, and playmate. The researchers found that in each dyad the older children assumed the dominant role when playing with a younger child. When older children played with a best friend, however, they demonstrated an egalitarian role. In the case of the triads, older children assumed a less dominant and more facilitative role.

Taken together, the findings of French and Brody et al. suggest that mixed-age groups benefit from positive affect from two sources — social perceptions and friendship.

Older children exhibit facilitative leadership

French, Waas, Stright, and Baker (1986) observed children's leadership roles. Children in mixed- and same-age groups were observed and interviewed during a decision-making process related to their classroom activities. The researchers studied verbal

> *Friendship appears to be a relationship that transcends age-related behavior.*

interaction, time on task, and similar classroom behaviors. Not surprisingly, older children were more likely to exhibit leadership behaviors than were younger children. The leadership behaviors were primarily those that facilitated group processes, for example, the solicitation of children's opinions. In fact, there was less opinion giving among older children in the mixed-age group than in the same-age group. For some children, leadership in the form of opinion giving is easier among younger than same-age peers.

Stright and French (1988) followed up this study to take a closer look at leadership behavior in groups of children seven and nine years old and nine and eleven years old. The researchers observed children in the process of reaching consensus on the appropriate order of a set of pictures. The observations showed that in the presence of younger children, nine-year-olds exhibited more organizing statements, solicitations of preferences, and group choice suggestions, and engaged in less following behavior than when they were with older children. According to Stright and French, the older children in the mixed-age groups facilitated and organized the participation of younger children "and did not utilize simple dominance to control the decision" (1988, p. 513). They point out, "Many children do not possess the skills and characteristics that enable them to emerge as a leader in a group of peers. With sufficient age disparity, however, any child can attain leadership status with younger children" (p. 513). Therefore, mixed-age groups provide appropriate contexts in which children can practice leadership skills.

Prosocial behaviors

Prosocial behaviors are often treated as indexes of social competence. These behaviors, such as help giving, sharing, and turn taking, facilitate interaction in the group setting and promote socialization.

*For some children, leadership is easier among younger than
same-age peers.*

12/THE CASE FOR MIXED-AGE GROUPING

> *Prosocial behaviors are often treated as indexes of social competence. These behaviors, such as help giving, sharing, and turn taking, facilitate interaction in the group setting and promote socialization.*

Mixed-age groups enhance older children's responsibility

In a study of peer interaction in mixed-age groups of first and third graders, Graziano, French, Brownell, and Hartup (1976) assessed social competence through a cooperative task (building with blocks) in which triads of mixed- and single-age children participated. They studied both group and individual performances in the two kinds of groups. Individual performance was assessed by the number of blocks a child used in his or her building, the kind of vocalizations used, who placed the first block, and who straightened the blocks. Group performance measures included these variables as well as the number of blocks that fell and alterations made by members of the group. The individual's performance differed according to the age composition of the specific triad. In particular, older children seemed to accept more responsibility than did younger children for the triad's overall performance. Children in a mixed-age triad demonstrated overall task awareness and showed sensitivity by assuming responsibility for task completion when the triad included younger children. Graziano et al. (1976) suggest that older children might be more sensitive to the complexity of interaction when they are in mixed- rather than in single-age groups. Initiative and assumption of responsibility may accommodate the group's building task when children perceive themselves as more proficient builders.

Children appear to play as freely in mixed-age as same-age groups

Lougee, Grueneich, and Hartup (1977), assessing spontaneous positive and negative social behaviors, observed preschoolers and kindergartners together during free play sessions in homogeneous and mixed-age groups. Positive social behaviors included spontaneous attention to peers, affection, submission (yielding), and reciprocation. Negative social behaviors were derogations, interferences, noncompliances, and attacks. The appropriateness of children's verbal interaction and the time they devoted to a given task (free play or play with a board game) were also studied. The amount of social interaction did not seem to vary according to the ages of the children.

Self-regulation appears to improve

In a review of research related to non-age-mate peer relationships, Lougee and Graziano (1986) point out that when children are cast in the role of rule enforcer, their subsequent self-regulation appears to improve. Thus, when older children in a mixed-age class are encouraged to remind younger ones of the rules, their own self-regulation may be enhanced. Lougee and Graziano suggest that acting as a rule enforcer may be one of several ways in which children learn to obey rules and to control their own behavior, indicating the "joint influence of age relationships and the role requirements that facilitate the development of self-regulation" (1986, p. 23). They also point out that the role of mixed-age rule enforcement may be useful for a child who is having difficulty learning to comply with the rules. Thus, if older children who are resistant to adult authority are encouraged to assist younger ones in observing the routines and rules of the setting, the older children may become more compliant themselves.

Group participation

Children's frequency and type of participation in group-related activities vary with the group composition, as well as with the nature of the activity.

Social participation is heightened for younger children

To examine the effect of mixed-age interaction on social participation, Goldman (1981) studied three- and four-year-old children in mixed-age groups that formed spontaneously in the classroom. By using an adapted form of Parten's (1933) play categories, Gold-

Younger children can engage in more interactive and complex types of play when older peers are easily accessible to them than when they are in homogeneous age groups.

> *When older children in a mixed-age class are encouraged to remind younger ones of the rules, their own self-regulation may be enhanced.*

man observed that younger children spent less time engaged in parallel play and required less teacher direction when in mixed-age triads. Goldman suggests that this finding has important implications for the design and organization of environments for young children. Specifically, younger children can engage in more interactive and complex types of play when older peers are easily accessible to them than when they are in homogeneous age groups.

Older children create complex play for younger ones

Similarly, Howes and Farver (1987) examined the complexity of social pretend play in an investigation of the social participation of two- and five-year-olds playing in a mixed group. Two categories of social pretend play were used. *Simple* social pretend play was scored when both participants engaged in pretend actions. *Cooperative* social pretend play required the participants to assume complementary roles such as mother-baby or driver-passenger. The study included observations of children's communications about play, teaching, attempts to direct play, and imitation. Howes and Farver observed that two-year-olds engaged in more cooperative social pretend play with older peers than with same-age peers. However, they were "more effective in cooperating with an age-mate than with an older child, [suggesting] that children may be more assertive with younger children and with age-mates than with older children" (Howes & Farver, 1987, p. 311).

The researchers also compared the differential effects of asking a five-year-old to teach versus play with a two-year-old. In a mixed-age group, the toddler engages in complex pretend play "because the older partner has the skills to structure the roles for both partners. The toddler, limited in pretense and communicative skills, is less able to create the same complex play when interacting with age-mates" (Howes & Farver, 1987, p. 313). The authors suggest that child care centers that "serve toddlers as well as preschool-age children may modify their curricula to include op-

Child care centers that serve toddlers as well as preschool-age children may modify their curricula to include opportunities for structured, mixed-age interaction.

portunities for structured, mixed-age interaction" (p. 313). Cooperative social pretend play with more mature partners can help young children acquire new social skills and concepts as they are demonstrated through the emerging forms of social pretend play. For older children, interaction provides opportunities for practice and mastery of social skills. This happens because mixed-age grouping offers older children occasions to organize the play activities with and for less mature playmates. In a mixed-age class, dramatic play activities can yield benefits to all participants.

In a similar study, Mounts and Roopnarine (1987) compared the play patterns of three- and four-year-olds in mixed-age and same-age groups. Younger children in the mixed-age groups engaged in more complex play than did their peers in homogeneous age groups. They were able to participate in play situations too complex for them to initiate, but not too complex for them to participate in when a more competent child initiated the situation. Mounts and Roopnarine argue that one advantage of mixed-age classrooms is that for many children they have a closer resemblance to children's homes and the social milieu to which children are more accustomed than have age-segregated classes. When a caregiver creates environments at school that are similar to those at home, the resulting sense of continuity may ease many young children's adaptation to the school environment.

Older children operate well in younger children's "zone of proximal development"

The findings reported by Howes and Farver (1987) and Mounts and Roopnarine (1987) invoke Vygotsky's "zone of proximal development" as a useful explanatory concept. The "zone of proximal development" is "the distance between the actual developmental level as determined by independent problem-solving and the level of potential development as determined through problem-solving under adult guidance or in collaboration with more capable peers" (as cited in Wertsch, 1985, p. 24). The adult's guidance has been referred to as "scaffolding." According to Brown and Palincsar (1986), the "metaphor of a scaffold captures the idea of an adjustable and temporary support than can be removed when no longer necessary" (p. 35). In the studies cited here, the older children in the mixed-age groups appear to provide scaffolding for the play of the younger ones (Wertsch, 1985) and in this sense operate within the younger children's zone of proximal de-

> *Mixed-age groupings may provide*
> *therapeutic or remedial benefits to*
> *children in certain kinds of "at risk"*
> *categories.*

velopment or "region of sensitivity to instruction" (Brown & Palincsar, 1986, p. 148). A more extensive discussion of the zone of proximal development is presented in Chapter 3.

Therapeutic effects of mixed-age interaction

Several studies of children's behavior in mixed-age groups suggest that such groupings may provide therapeutic or remedial benefits to children in certain kinds of "at risk" categories. It has been established, for example, that children are more likely to exhibit prosocial behavior (Whiting, 1983) and offer instruction (Brody, Stoneman, & MacKinnon, 1982; Ludeke & Hartup, 1983) to younger children than to age-mates. They are more likely to establish friendships (Hartup, 1976) and exhibit aggression (Whiting & Whiting, 1975) with age-mates. They usually imitate older children (Brody et al., 1982) and display dependency on them.

Younger children allow isolated older children social skills practice

The therapeutic effects of mixed-age interaction are indicated in a study by Furman, Rahe, and Hartup (1979) in which withdrawn preschool children participated in mixed-age groups for rehabilitative purposes. These children were paired with younger and with same-age children. They were compared to a same-age control group. The preschoolers who interacted with younger children made the greatest gains in sociability. The results suggest that lack of leadership skills may be a cause of social isolation. When older isolated children had an opportunity to interact with younger children, they could practice leadership skills. This study has significant implications in light of the enormous concern about the social adjustment of many children.

In a three-week intervention program, Kim (1990) assigned 12 rejected-aggressive and 12 rejected-withdrawn preschool children to three conditions: play sessions in dyads with a socially average younger child, play dyads with a peer, and no treatment. Following the intervention, the rejected children who had experienced the cross-age-interaction dyads were more often nominated as friends by their classmates compared to rejected children in dyads with a peer or without treatment. These results persisted in a follow-up assessment three weeks after the intervention program.

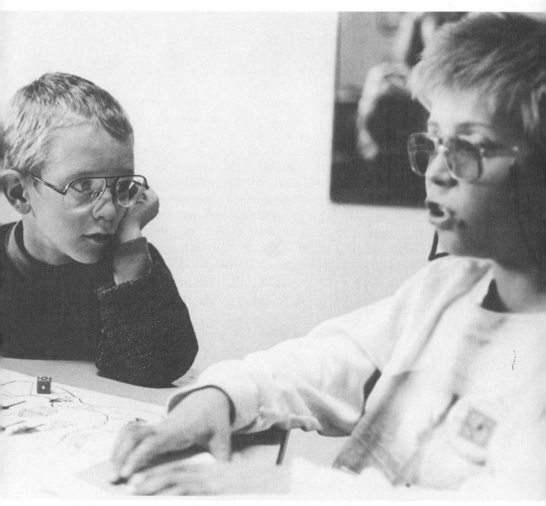

Both younger and older children in mixed-age groups differentiate their behavior and vary their expectations, depending on the ages of the participants.

Such encouraging findings from a very brief treatment suggest that young children experiencing social difficulties may benefit from extensive opportunity for cross-age interaction in a naturalistic setting like a classroom environment.

It seems reasonable to expect that the availability of younger and therefore less threatening classmates in mixed-age groups offers the possibility of remedial or therapeutic effects for children whose social development is "at risk." In fact, the leadership that older children exhibit in mixed-age groups (French et al., 1986) is recognized as one of the social skills involved in improving general ability to develop social relationships (Mize & Ladd, in press). Modeling, reinforcement for social approach, social perspective taking, and social skill training have been used with varying degrees of success (Mize & Ladd, in press). In all of these remedial programs, the adults have played the role of reinforcer and trainer. However, the concepts are difficult for trainers to teach young children directly. It seems reasonable that a preschooler who has little confidence in his own social skills might be more easily rebuffed by age-mates than by younger, less socially mature children. Thus, social interaction with younger, less socially sophisticated classmates might give children with such low confidence opportunities to practice and refine their interactive skills in a relatively accepting social environment. The potential benefits of mixed-age groups for children with social difficulties may depend upon the nature of the specific difficulties addressed, however. The benefits may be greater for children who are isolated than for those who are rejected by peers because of their aggressive tendencies.

Summary of social effects research

The evidence discussed thus far suggests that children of different ages are usually aware of the differences and attributes associated with age. Consequently, both younger and older children in mixed-age groups differentiate their behavior and vary their expectations, depending on the ages of the participants. Mixed-age group interaction elicits specific prosocial behaviors such as helping, sharing, and taking turns, which are important in young children's social development. Mixed-age groups provide older children with leadership opportunities, which may be especially important for some at-risk children, and provide younger children with opportunities for more complex pretend play than they could initiate themselves.

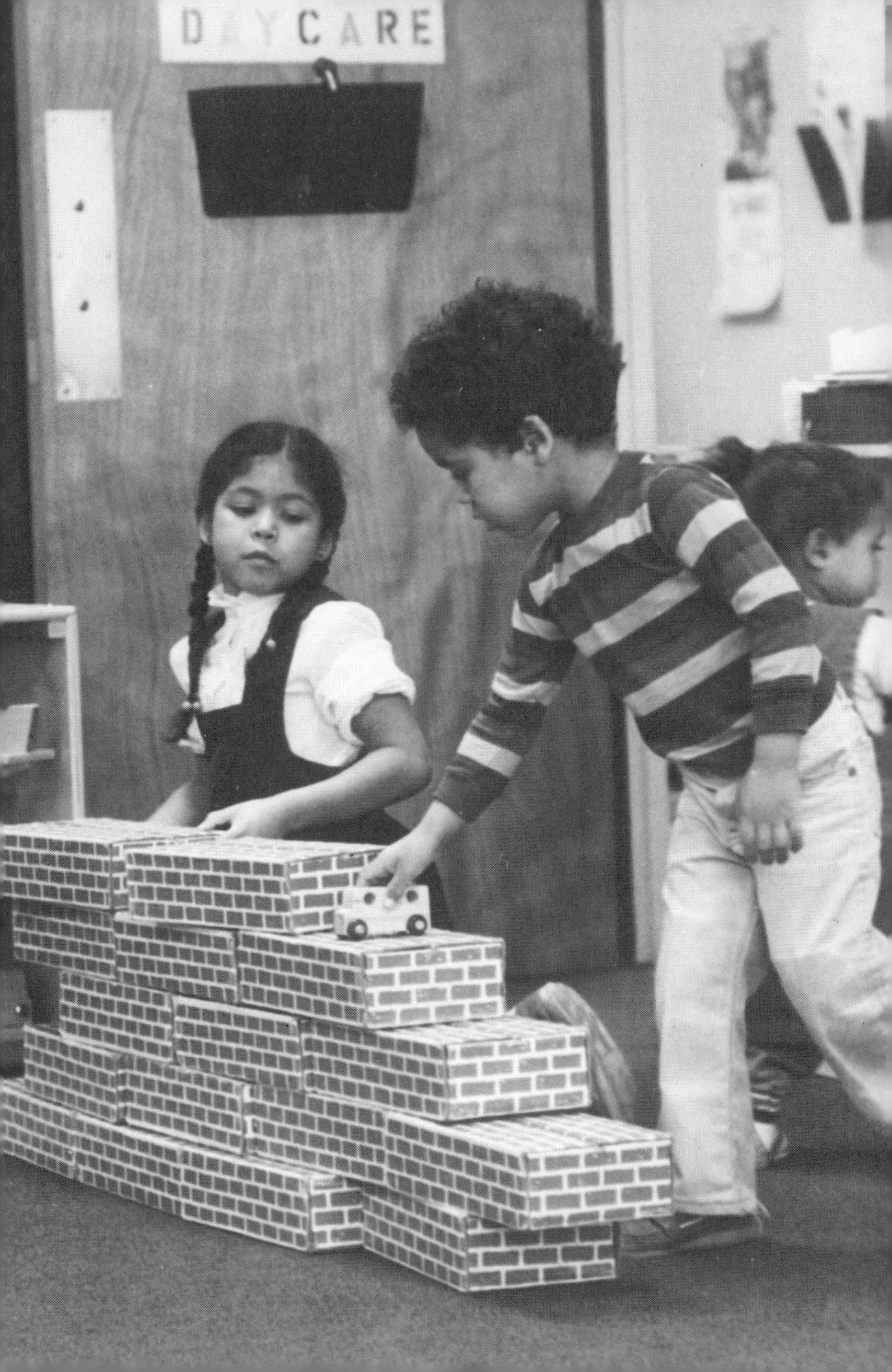
DAYCARE

Chapter 3

Cognitive Basis for Mixed-Age Grouping

S TUDIES RELATED TO MIXED-AGE GROUPING AND COGNITIVE DEVEL-OPMENT SUGGEST THAT COGNITIVE CONFLICT IN A CHILD ARISES FROM his interaction with children of different levels of cognitive maturity. It is assumed that optimal cognitive conflict stimulates cognitive growth by challenging participants to assimilate and accommodate to the new information represented by their differences in understanding.

Effective cognitive conflict from peer interaction

Brown and Palincsar (1986) make the point that such conflict's contribution to learning is not simply that the less informed child imitates the more knowledgeable one. The interactions between those who hold conflicting understandings lead the less informed member to internalize new understandings in the form of "fundamental cognitive restructuring" (p. 31). Along the same lines, Vygotsky (1978) maintains that internalization occurs when concepts are actually transformed and not merely replicated. Thus, the kinds of cognitive conflict likely to arise during cross-age interaction provide contexts for significant learning for younger children as they strive to accommodate to the different understandings presented by older classmates. For example, in an experiment on conservation, Botwin and Murray (1975) demonstrated that non-conservers gained significantly in conservation

> *The interactions between those who hold conflicting understandings lead the less informed member to internalize new understandings in the form of "fundamental cognitive restructuring."*

of number, mass, weight, and amount by either observing conservers or engaging in resolution through social conflict. Similar results have been difficult to replicate, however.

Cognitive conflict is a complex condition

The precise cognitive stage and the socialization patterns of those involved must also be considered: specifically, the perspectives of both children as well as the conditions under which conflict occurs (Tudge, 1986a, 1986b). As Brown and Palincsar (1986) point out, a child can learn effectively from another only when the less informed child already has a partial grasp of the concept in question. In other words, for cognitive conflict to be effective, the concepts being learned must exist between the points of the child's actual and potential ability or, in Vygotsky's term, within the child's "zone of proximal development."

Slavin (1987) points out that the discrepancy between what an individual can do with and without assistance can be the basis for cooperative efforts that can result in cognitive gains. In his view, "collaborative activity among children promotes growth because children of similar ages are likely to be operating within one another's proximal zones of development, modeling in the collaborating group behaviors more advanced than those they could perform as individuals" (p. 1162). The work of Slavin and others in cooperative learning procedures does not specifically address age differences among members of cooperative groups. Nevertheless, the research available on the application and effectiveness of cooperative learning supports the view that many of the differences between members of learning groups can be used for socially and intellectually desirable goals.

The discrepancy between what an individual can do with and without assistance can be the basis for cooperative efforts that can result in cognitive gains.

"Novices" and "experts" in mixed-age groups

If learning tasks involve children working together instead of individually or competitively, fruitful collaboration between "novices" and "experts" can occur. Research by Brown, Bransford, Ferrara, and Campione (1983) and Brown and Reeve (1985) supports Vygotsky's contention that learning experiences are most likely to enhance development when children's activities are socially directed by "experts." Experts are more capable people who provide prompts to increasingly advanced solutions, direct leading questions, and cause "novices" to defend or alter their theories. The notion that supportive social contexts create new levels of competence, then, defends the use of mixed-age grouping, in which ranges of competence offer varying levels of cognitive input.

In a study of peer collaboration, Azmitia (1988) examined problem solving. The children in the study were not mixed in age, but they were selected specifically as "novices" and "experts" on a given task. Such novices and experts may be considered analogous to the competence differences that exist among children of different ages. Azmitia found that experts, even at the preschool level, positively influenced novices' learning by offering information, guidance, and new viewpoints and affected novice children's acquisition of cognitive and social skills such as negotiation, argumentation, and cooperative work skills.

Children adjust communication for listeners

Communicative competence also makes a significant contribution to cognitive development (Gelman & Baillargeon, 1983). In research involving communication skills and syntactic adjustment, Shatz and Gelman (1973) grouped three- and four-year-olds

> *The notion that supportive social contexts create new levels of competence defends the use of mixed-age grouping, in which ranges of competence offer varying degrees of cognitive support.*

together. They studied the children's ability to alter their linguistic behavior according to the age of the listeners. Sentence length and complexity differed depending on the listener's age. Shatz and Gelman's findings support the hypothesis that children are sensitive to the age and assumed level of verbal ability of the listener and adjust their verbal behavior accordingly. Furthermore, the closer the speaker's age was to that of the listener, the fewer adjustments the speaker made. Shatz and Gelman conclude that communication, being an interactive process, requires participants to adjust to each other in order to create a favorable communicative environment.

In another study of mixed groups of preschoolers and kindergartners (Lougee, Gruenich, & Hartup, 1977), the younger children's linguistic maturity, measured by the length of utterance, improved as they addressed older peers. No significant improvement was reported for older children.

Summary

Psychologists and educators do not yet fully understand how mixed-age interaction affects cognitive development. More data are needed. Nevertheless, the concepts of cognitive conflict and the zone of proximal development provide some theoretical justification for experimenting with education in mixed-age grouping in the early years.

The implication of the theory and research is that careful consideration must be given to the precise conditions under which benefits of cognitive conflict can be fully realized. Structuring learning tasks so that "novices" and "experts" can collaborate is one promising approach. More research is needed on the interactive processes involved and the teacher's role in them.

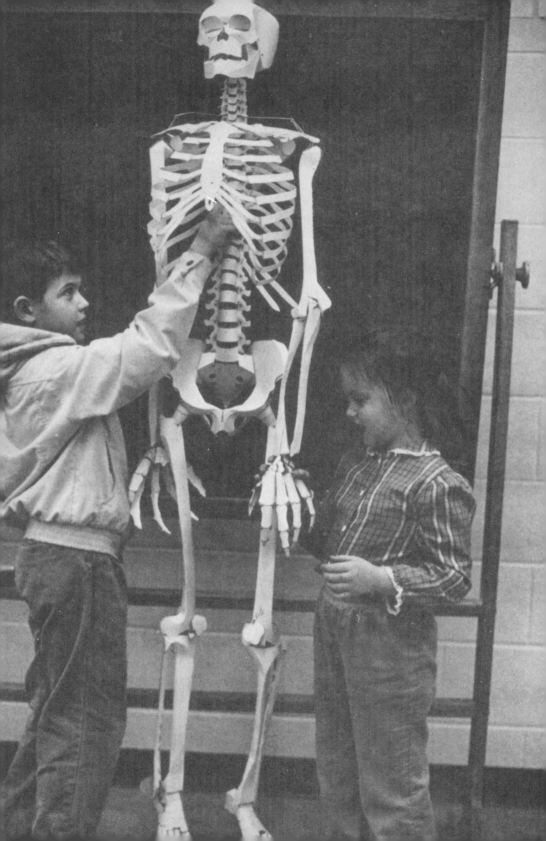

Chapter 4

Strategies for Mixed-Age Learning: Peer Tutoring and Cooperative Learning

ALTHOUGH DEVELOPMENTAL RESEARCH RELATED TO MIXED-AGE GROUPING IS RATHER LIMITED IN SCOPE AND SIZE, AND THE CONclusions are still tentative, research on the strategies of childchild tutoring and cooperative learning is extensive. While the research on these two subjects is not specifically focused on children's ages, it appears to have clear implications for mixed-age group learning experiences.

Peer tutoring

Peer tutoring is defined as a "one-to-one teaching process in which the tutor is of the same general academic status as the tutee" (Cohen, 1986, p. 175). Cohen suggests that both the tutor and the tutee gain academically and interpersonally through the interaction. The exposure to and rehearsal of the material, and the presentation and concentration on the lessons, involve the active participation of both members.

There being some cognitive closeness in peer tutoring suggests that the tutor can operate in the tutee's "zone of proximal development" (Slavin, 1987). Learning is facilitated because the distance between peer tutors' and tutees' understandings is smaller than the distance between the understandings of children and adults. In a sense, adults teach well because they can intentionally overcome the great cognitive distance between themselves and young children. Furthermore, the tutors are thought to be more sensitive and empathetic than teachers to the predicament of the tutees. The tutor is less likely than an experienced teacher to have firmly formed self-fulfilling prophecies and expectations about the interaction's outcome. Of course, some children are more competent tutors than others.

In an analysis of 65 studies of school tutoring programs, Cohen, Kulik, and Kulik (1982) found that the majority had a positive effect on the tutees' academic performance and attitudes toward tutoring. Twenty-eight of these studies involved mixed-age tutoring.

Lippitt (1976) suggests that cross-age tutoring is actually an extension of human beings' natural tendency to interact with and learn from those who are older and more knowledgeable. Both younger and older children can benefit from tutoring. Younger children can be enriched by individualized instruction from older children; the latter learn in reviewing the material to be taught and in performing competently during tutoring. These experiences also increase many tutors' self-confidence and sense of worth.

Tutoring offers both tutor and tutee firsthand experience of the teaching and learning process, which can be useful in modifying attitudes toward learning and studying. It gives participants an opportunity to experience schooling from the perspective of tutor as well as learner. Tutoring also benefits teachers because it provides additional instruction in the classroom.

Cooperative learning structures

As indicated by several studies, peer tutoring encompasses many elements found in cooperative learning (Russell & Ford, 1983; Johnson, Johnson, Holubec, & Roy, 1984; Slavin, 1987). Cooperative learning involves children in face-to-face interaction and in sharing responsibility for learning. It also involves shared leadership and positive interdependence among group members. Individual accountability is likewise crucial in promoting achievement in these groups (Johnson et al., 1984).

Peer tutoring is defined as a "one-to-one teaching process in which the tutor is of the same general academic status as the tutee."

In a meta-analysis of 122 studies on the comparative effects of cooperative, competitive, and individualistic goal structures on achievement, it has been found that cooperation is by far the most effective in enhancing achievement.

In an analysis of 122 studies on the comparative effects of cooperative, competitive, and individualistic goal structures on achievement, Johnson et al. concluded that cooperation is by far the most effective in enhancing achievement. In view of the larger issues of social adjustment, and given the increasing concern with children's motivation, the search for goal structures that enhance learning and prosocial development is timely.

Lew, Mesch, Johnson, and Johnson (1986) demonstrated the effects of cooperative learning on positive interdependence. Isolated children experienced gains in achievement, in interpersonal attraction, and in the use of collaborative skills in cooperative learning groups. The researchers contend that the isolated children's acquisition and application of collaborative skills during the cooperative learning activities developed their self-confidence, which in turn resulted in more interaction with peers. Therefore, cooperative learning may bring many children with social difficulties into a positive *recursive cycle* (Katz, 1988) in which their acceptance by others leads to greater confidence in approaching them, greater acceptance increases their confidence, and this, in turn, increases their acceptance by peers.

Although the cooperative learning approach is not directly concerned with the participants' ages, it is related to the use of the differences between participants in the service of learning. The maximization of differences between participants is one of the rationales for our recommendation of mixed-age grouping in early childhood education settings.

Summary

Although empirical data on the educational principles that should guide instruction in mixed-age environments are not yet available, we propose that the principles of cooperative goal structures (Ames & Ames, 1984) and peer tutoring could be useful in mixed-age situations. Under classroom conditions marked by co-operative (versus competitive) goal structures, a range of competence in all developmental domains that concern teachers is accepted. Furthermore, substantial evidence indicates that children's motivation is increased when working in cooperative learning groups and that that can improve the quality and equality in relationships and achievement in education (Nicholls, 1979).

Chapter 5

Mixed-Age Settings: Some Successful Examples

Research evidence regarding mixed-age grouping is complemented by the existence of mixed-age programs both in the United States and other countries. Historically, the Progressive Education movement in this country fostered multi-age grouping. The most extensive contemporary use of mixed-age grouping has been in the British infant schools for children five to seven years old.

In an experimental program to examine the effects of cross-age interaction on social behavior, Roopnarine (1987) implemented a summer preschool program at the University of Wisconsin Mixed-Age Laboratory School. The program's first objective was to provide children with

> ample opportunity for observational learning, imitation, and tutoring, and to provide the environment for engaging in simple to complex modes of cognitive and social play. Older children would be provided the opportunities to sharpen skills already learned, while younger children would be exposed to the behaviors of more competent older peers. (p. 147)

The second objective was to give teachers experience in implementing a curriculum for mixed-age groups. The teachers were required to develop lesson plans that "would lead to group participation and cohesion rather than social segregation" (p. 148). Roopnarine describes the curriculum as having an "open classroom" orientation, offering the range of activi-

> *Research evidence regarding mixed-age grouping is complemented by the existence of mixed-age programs both in the United States and other countries. Historically, the Progressive Education movement in this country has fostered multi-age grouping.*

ties and experiences associated with traditional nursery and kindergarten education.

On the basis of his findings, Roopnarine proposes that mixed-age classrooms can indeed function as an instructional and curricular model because they yield increased levels of cooperation and greater complexity of interaction than do single-age classrooms.

> Across a range of social/cognitive constructs and in different settings, children appear quite sensitive to their peers' ages. The mixed-age grouping appears to elicit a number of social behaviors among children of varying developmental status. Thus, cross-age peer relations may serve various adaptive functions that are central to the process of cognitive and social development. (Roopnarine, 1987, p. 147)

These adaptive functions, which are examined in a number of studies, involve play behaviors, language modification, and social rehabilitation.

University of Northern Iowa Malcolm Price Laboratory School

Since the mid-1970s, the Malcolm Price Laboratory School has operated a two-year kindergarten that mixes four- and five-year-olds. The program operates on the assumption that "the greater the difference among children in a classroom, the richer the learning environment for the child" (Doud & Finkelstein, 1985, p. 9). These authors assert that the mixed-age kindergarten has many advantages. Mixed-age grouping allows richer verbal behavior and better language development, the enhanced self-confidence needed to master new tasks, and opportunities to achieve developmental potentials. Additional benefits are opportunities for immature five-year-olds and mature four-year-olds to interact at similar developmental levels and the minimization of retention of children deemed unready for first grade (and thus the social stigma that often goes with retention). Doud and Finkelstein (1985) also suggest that the teachers' having two years with each child is an asset of the program.

Although these authors claim that the Malcolm Price Laboratory School has been successful, they provide little specific information about the curriculum and not much data to support claims of success. They do caution, however, that it would be a major error to integrate four-year-olds into kindergartens that formally teach reading and writing and that place premiums on basic academic skills rather than in-depth learning. The key function of the mixed-age kindergarten is to augment general intellectual growth rather than to accelerate the acquisition of isolated academic skills.

Fajans School in Sweden

The practice of mixed-age grouping is common in other countries, especially in locations where the numbers in each age cohort are too small to constitute a whole class. Papadopoulos (1988) describes the Fajans School in Sweden, in which 220 elementary-age children were not organized into age or ability groups.

> Children at [the school] are not graded according to age. They belong, instead, to a colour unit. In each unit there is a nursery department, a junior class and an intermediate class. Ages in each colour unit range from 9 months to 12 years. Each colour unit has its own team or staff, including teachers, recreation leaders and some kitchen and cleaning staff. There is full co-operation between the staff and the children of the various units of the planning and organization of the various school activities. (p. 3)

According to Papadopoulos's report, the school's objectives are to create close contact between the preschool and primary units, to create a homelike atmosphere, and to maintain the same peer groups from the nursery to the primary years. Papadopoulos points out that even the physical facilities are designed to encourage the achievement of these objectives. For example, there is no large dining room because the children eat in their rooms. The building is designed to "facilitate flexibility and free movement of pupils in the classrooms" (p. 4), and each classroom has "a cosy

It would be a major error to integrate four-year-olds into kindergartens that formally teach reading and writing and that place premiums on basic academic skills rather than in-depth learning.

> *At the beginning of each school year, 10 new pupils replace the old ones.*

reading area with comfortable chairs and ample bookshelves for working materials and a large area where pupils can work in small groups" (p. 4). Teachers collaborate in regular planning meetings alternating within and across grade levels. Each class contains children from the three grades. At the beginning of each school year, 10 new pupils of the youngest grade replace ten of the oldest ones: "Thus, no teacher is faced with the problem of having 30 new pupils every third year" (p. 4). Based on the brief description of the school, the curriculum appears to offer a mixture of formal, informal, spontaneous, and assigned activities similar to those recommended by Katz and Chard (1989).

> Pupils collaborate across "school borders" working on practical themes. Also classes from the main school work together with the nursery school to organize various activities, such as traffic training, woodland paths, story times, etc. (Papadopoulos, 1988, p. 4)

The description of the school's atmosphere and of the children's work suggests that, while mixed-age grouping is only one aspect of this school, it is one that contributes substantially to the "warmth, openness, friendliness ... freedom of movement, freedom of exchange of ideas" (p. 5) noted by the observers. Unfortunately, the report does not include descriptions of the implementation of these arrangements in greater detail than cited above.

Summary

Mixed-age group interaction can have unique adaptive, facilitating, and enriching effects on children's development (Lougee & Graziano, undated; Graziano et al., 1976; Hartup, 1983). Mixed-age grouping programs demonstrate the advantages and possibilities of the practice. The programs' existence indicates that the idea is neither novel nor rare, and indeed it may be an idea whose time has come, given recent trends in childrearing and family size, the increasing lengths of time children spend in child care outside of the home, and the increasing academic demands on young children in preschools and kindergartens.

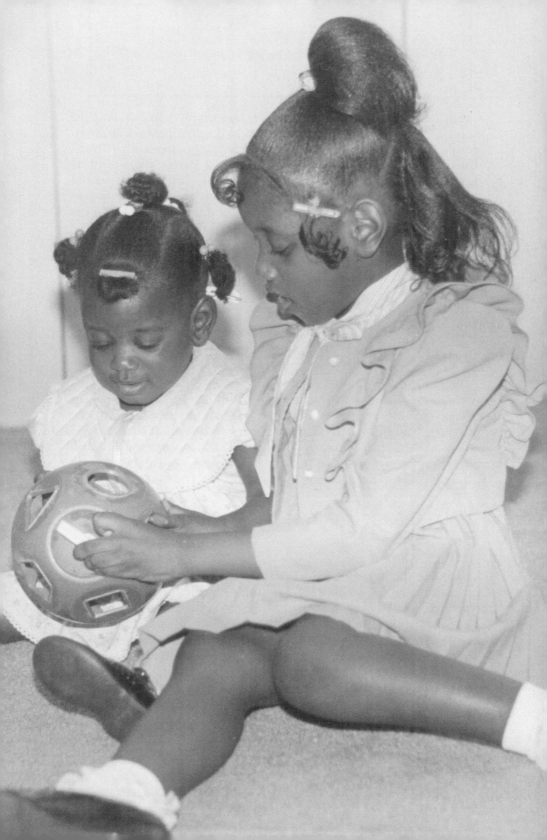

Chapter 6

Questions About Implementing Mixed-Age Grouping

Rescearch indicates that cross-age interaction among young children can offer a variety of developmental benefits to all participants. However, merely mixing children of different ages in a group will not guarantee that the benefits described in the preceding discussion will be realized. Four areas of concern are the optimum age range, the proportion of older to younger children, the time allocated to mixed-age grouping, and the appropriate curriculum. None of these concerns has been examined by empirical studies. We attempt here a preliminary exploration of questions.

What is the optimum age range?

Although no systematic evidence has been found concerning the beneficial effects of the age range within a group, experience suggests that the range is likely to affect the group in several ways. We hypothesize that there is an *optimal* age range and that children too far apart in age will not engage in enough interaction to affect each other. If the age span within a group goes beyond the optimal range, then the models of behavior and competence exhibited by the oldest members may be too difficult for younger members to emulate. Indeed, there may be a risk that the eldest children will intimidate the youngest members. Furthermore, we suggest that customary age-segregation practices provide too narrow a range of competence for maximum learning across much of the curriculum. For example, in a class composed entirely of three-year-olds, the children may not be able to engage in play as complex as they would engage in if in a class including four-year-olds. However, in many schools and child care centers, the mixture of age groups is more likely to be determined by the actual enrollments than by empirically derived formulae.

Research is needed to illuminate the dynamic factors that operate in various age ranges. Comparative studies of classes with a two- versus a three-year age spread could identify the effects of age range on the frequencies, structure, and content of cross-age interaction. It would also be useful to know whether the types and frequencies of prosocial behaviors (e.g., nurturance, leadership, tutoring) that older children exhibit in interactions with younger ones are related to the spread in ages. Of course, in many situations, the age range may not be a matter of choice, but rather a function of demographic factors beyond the school's control. The advantages or risks associated with age ranges are not clear from any available data.

What is the best proportion of older to younger children in a class?

There is at present no empirical basis on which to predict what proportions of older to younger children within a class are optimal. Real conditions are unlikely to allow teachers to have one-half the class age four and the other half age five. It seems likely that if the class consists of five four-year-olds and 15 five-year-olds, the youngest members might easily be overwhelmed by their older classmates. However, if the proportions are reversed, might the demands of the younger children overshadow the needs of the older ones, and the acceptance of behavior appropriate from the younger children give the older ones license to behave in these less mature ways as well? In either case, the teacher's role includes not only fostering cooperative and constructive interaction across the age groups, but also minimizing the potential risks of the uneven distribution of the age groups and the kinds of behavioral characteristics associated with them. We have only indirectly related evidence on these issues — from cross-cultural studies on peer interaction (Whiting & Whiting, 1975). The Whitings' classical study describes a wide age range of peer interaction found in other

Merely mixing children of different ages in a group will not guarantee that the benefits described in the preceding discussion will be realized. Four areas of concern are the optimum age range, the proportion of older to younger children, the time allocated to mixed-age grouping, and the appropriate curriculum.

cultures. The Whitings report that prosocial behaviors tend to emerge, and relationships among children of all ages are characterized by cooperation.

What proportion of time ought to be spent in mixed-age groups?

There is as yet no evidence to indicate what proportion of the time children spend in an early childhood setting should be spent in mixed-age groups. However, we might consider possible mixtures of ages in early childhood settings and elementary schools. An ideal elementary school that has provisions for four-year-olds could be organized to provide an early childhood section or department for children four to six years old. (The National Association of State Boards of Education, 1988, recommends a unit composed of four- to eight-year-olds.) In such an early childhood department, the children might spend all of their time in mixed groups, depending to a large extent on the nature of the curriculum. If the curriculum is mainly informal and includes spontaneous play, learning centers, project work, and individual assignments as needed, children's progress in acquiring basic literacy and numeracy skills will not be jeopardized.

Another plan might be to set aside particular periods during which the teacher offers specific learning and instructional activities for small, flexible sub-groups of children with relatively homogeneous abilities, knowledge, or competence. Members of these groups might work on specific individual assignments and receive systematic instruction as needed. While these small groups are receiving special instruction (see Katz & Chard, 1989, pp. 10–11), others in the class can continue to work on projects or play together in spontaneous groups.

On the other hand, a school might want to have a home room for several periods of the day. For example, the children might be in mixed-age groups during an opening period, an extended lunch and rest time at midday, and perhaps during the last half-hour of school. The main advantages to the age mixture in this arrangement stem from opportunity for social interaction rather than from various kinds of cross-age tutoring or mixed-age project work.

The teaching staff of an early childhood department can allocate some time each day that cooperative learning groups use to work

> *Efforts to maximize family grouping seem to be especially appropriate in child care centers in which many young children spend the majority of their waking hours.*

on assigned learning tasks. We suggest that the staff plan together the allocation of time and their own efforts in such a way that a balanced grouping results. When such a balance exists, mixed- and same-age groups have the opportunity to form spontaneously, and the teacher can organize assigned groups (more or less mixed in age) for specific instructional purposes. Each child would spend her first three years in the department, participating in a variety of peer groups. In this way, the uneven development and progress of many young children could be addressed by the flexibility of placement both in same-age and within mixed-age groups.

Efforts to maximize family grouping seem to be especially appropriate in child care centers in which many young children spend the majority of their waking hours. A class in a center could be composed of three-, four-, and five-year-olds. The early part of their day could be spent participating together in the morning meal. The children could take a real role, appropriate to their level of competence, in setting the table and cleaning up after the meal, and could undertake real household chores before starting to play. Of course, the group does not have to be mixed in age to create this kind of family or community atmosphere. This plan would enhance the homelike quality of child care settings and reduce the temptation to "scholarize" the lives of very young children in child care. If, as is often the case, their siblings are enrolled in the center, increasing the opportunities for sibling contact is desirable. Many young children in institutions may find contact with siblings during the day a source of comfort.

Thus far, there are no data that suggest the optimal allocation of time to mixed- versus homogeneous-age grouping. There is therefore no reason to believe that time must be allocated to either one or the other age-grouping arrangement. Maximizing the advantages and minimizing the risks of mixed-age grouping and making proper use of time will depend largely on the judgment and skillfulness of the teacher.

What about curriculum and mixed-age groups?

One of the possible benefits of mixing ages in the early childhood classroom may be a reduction of teachers' and administrators' tendency to adopt a unidimensional curriculum consisting of exercises and assignments that all children must complete within a given time. Instead of a formal academic curriculum for a whole class or age cohort, we recommend an informal curriculum with ample group project work, opportunity for spontaneous play, and systematic instruction for individual children as needed.

Children might spend all of their time in mixed groups, depending to a large extent on the nature of the curriculum.

Unless the curriculum has a significant amount of time allocated to informal group work and spontaneous interactive play in naturally occurring groups, the benefits of the age spread are unlikely to be realized. Katz and Chard (1989) propose that the curriculum for all young children should include opportunities for children to work on extended group projects in which individuals contribute differentially to the effort at many levels of competence.

If a class includes five- and six-year-olds in a family grouping arrangement, some fives will be closer to six-year-olds than to other fives in a given skill and will profit from small-group instruction that involves six-year-olds as well. Similarly, some six-year-olds may benefit from small-group experiences that involve certain activities with five-year-olds for a while. The composition of the groups can be fluid, depending on the tasks and the rate of progress of each child.

One of the important potential advantages of a mixed-age early childhood department is the minimization of grade retention and repetition. Any child who had spent two or three years in such a department and was still judged unable to unlikely to profit from the subsequent grade, which might be called Year 1 of primary school, could be referred for special services. Any curriculum for which more than 10% of the age-eligible children are judged unready is probably inappropriate (Katz, Raths, & Torres, 1987; Graue & Shepard, 1989).

Summary

Although mixed-age grouping is a straightforward concept, the practical details of implementation are not well researched. Experience and some research, however, suggest that 1) an optimum age range is larger than the customary range in current classrooms, yet not so wide that children cannot share interests, 2) the proportion of older to younger children should be large enough to keep the older children from regressing, 3) no particular proportion of time needs to be allocated to mixed- and same-age grouping, and 4) an informal, multidimensional, non-age-based curriculum is most appropriate to a mixed-age group.

Conclusion and Recommendations

THE RESEARCH REVIEWED SUGGESTS THAT MULTI-AGE GROUPING IN EARLY CHILDHOOD SETTINGS MAY BENEFIT PARTICIPANTS BY PROviding contexts for interaction in which a variety of models of behavior and levels of social, intellectual, and academic competences are available. It is assumed that a range of competences within a mixed-age group gives rise to cognitive conflicts and opportunities to lead, instruct, nurture, and strengthen skills and knowledge already acquired in the course of tutoring others. Thus, a mixed-age group is potentially a very rich educative environment.

Mixed-age grouping is especially desirable for young children who spend the majority of their waking hours in child care programs. In such environments family- and sibling-like relationships can be fostered and become a source of affection, comfort, and closeness for all children involved. Mixed-age grouping in the early years of elementary school can minimize the need for grade retention, repetition, and segregated classes for children deemed "unready" for the next grade.

Special benefits may also accrue to the teachers of mixed-age groups. It seems likely, for example, that the wider range of maturity available in mixed-age groups, compared to single-age groups, would decrease younger children's dependence upon the teacher for attention and assistance; more mature children can be sources of both. Similarly, for a variety of tasks and chores, older helpers are available to the youngest members. This expanded availability of help is likely to be especially beneficial to the center staff, who are responsible for virtually all aspects of children's functioning throughout the long day.

Clearly more research is needed, but evidence reported thus far gives us confidence in the value of developing appropriate curriculum and teaching strategies for mixed-age grouping in the early years.

On the basis of the foregoing we recommend that

- mixed-age grouping be implemented in classrooms serving young children
- curriculum be broadly conceived and designed so that teachers, principals, and parents understand that children working together are learning multidimensionally
- curriculum be oriented toward projects and activities that encourage and allow children to work collaboratively using the structures of peer tutoring, cooperative learning, and spontaneous grouping characteristic of young children's play settings
- teachers be provided with support and assistance in implementing mixed-age grouping because most current, sequential academic curricula do not support mixed-age grouping (the appendix supplies some suggestions to teachers)
- parents receive information and guidance about the benefits of mixed-age grouping as their children move into such experiences

References

Ames, C., & Ames, R. (1984). Goal structures and motivation. *The Elementary School Journal, 85*(1), 39–52.

Angus, D. L., Mirel, J. E., & Vinovskis, M. A. (1988). Historical development of age stratification in schooling. *Teachers College Record, 90*(2), 211–236.

Asher, S. R., & Parker, J. G. (in press). The significance of peer relationship problems in childhood. In B. H. Schneider, G. Attilli, J. Nadel, & R. P. Weissberg (Eds.), *Social competence in developmental perspective.* Amsterdam: Kluwer Academic Publishing.

Azmitia, M. (1988). Peer interaction and problem solving: When are two heads better than one? *Child Development, 59,* 87–96.

Botwin, G. J., & Murray, F. B. (1975). The efficacy of peer modeling and social conflict in the acquisition of conservation. *Child Development, 46,* 796–799.

Brody, G. H., Stoneman, Z., & MacKinnon, C. E. (1982). Role asymmetries in interaction among school aged children, their younger siblings and their friends. *Child Development, 53,* 1364–1370.

Brown, A. L., Bransford, J. D., Ferrara, R. A., & Campione, J. C. (1983). Learning, remembering, and understanding. In J. H. Flavell & E. M. Markman (Eds.), *Handbook of child psychology* (4th ed.). *Vol. 3: Cognitive development* (pp. 515–529). New York: Wiley.

Brown, A. L., & Palincsar A. (1986). *Guided, cooperative learning and individual knowledge acquisition* (Technical Report No, 372). Champaign, IL: Center for the Study of Reading.

Brown, A. L., & Reeve, R. A. (1985). *Bandwidths of competence: The role of supportive contexts in learning and development* (Technical Report No. 336). Champaign, IL: Center for the Study of Reading.

Clay, M. M. (1979). *The early detection of reading difficulties: A diagnostic survey with recovery procedures.* New Zealand: Heinemann.

Cohen, J. (1986). Theoretical considerations of peer tutoring. *Psychology in the Schools, 23,* 175–186.

Cohen, P. A., Kulik, S. A., & Kulik, C. C. (1982). Educational outcomes of tutoring: A meta-analysis of findings. *American Educational Research Journal, 19,* 237–248.

Connell, D. R. (1987, July). The first 30 years were the fairest: Notes from the kindergarten and ungraded primary (K–1–2). *Young Children, 42*(5), 30–39.

Doud, J. L., & Finkelstein, J. M. (1985). A two-year kindergarten that works. *Principal, 64*(5), 18–21.

Ellis, S., Rogoff, B., & Cromer, C. C. (1981). Age segregation in children's social interactions. *Developmental Psychology, 17,* 399–407.

French, D. C. (1984). Children's knowledge of the social functions of younger, older, and same age peers. *Child Development, 55,* 1429–1433.

French, D. C., Waas, G. A., Stright, A. L., & Baker, J. A. (1986). Leadership asymmetries in mixed-age children's groups. *Child Development, 57,* 1277–1283.

Furman, W., Rahe, D. F., & Hartup, W. W. (1979). Rehabilitation of socially withdrawn preschool children through mixed-age and same-age socialization. *Child Development, 50,* 915–922.

Gallagher, J. M., & Coche, J. (1987). Hothousing: The clinical and educational concerns over pressuring young children. *Early Childhood Research Quarterly, 2,* 203–210.

Gelman, R., & Baillargeon, R. (1983). A review of some Piagetian concepts. In P. H. Mussen (Ed.), *Handbook of child psychology* (4th ed.) *Vol. 3: Cognitive development* (pp. 167–230). New York: Wiley.

Gesell Institute of Human Development. (1982). *A gift of time.* New Haven, CT: Author.

Goldman, J. (1981). Social participation of preschool children in same versus mixed-age groups. *Child Development, 52,* 644–650.

Goodlad, J. I., & Anderson, R. H. (1959). *The non-graded elementary school.* New York: Teachers College Press, Columbia University.

Goodlad, J. I., & Anderson, R. H. (1987). *The non-graded elementary school* (rev. ed.). New York: Teachers College Press, Columbia University.

Graue, M. E., & Shepard, L. (1989). Predictive validity of Gesell School Readiness Tests. *Early Childhood Research Quarterly, 4,* 303–315.

Graziano, W. G., French, D., Brownell, C. A., & Hartup, W. W. (1976). Peer interaction in same-age and mixed-age triads in relation to chronological age and incentive condition. *Child Development, 47,* 707–714.

Greenberg, P. (1990). Why not academic preschool? (Part 1). *Young Children, 45*(2), 70–80.

Hartup, W. W. (1976). Cross-age versus same-age interaction: Ethological and cross-cultural perspectives. In V. L. Allen (Ed.), *Children as teachers: Theory and research on tutoring* (pp. 41–54). New York: Academic.

Hartup, W. W. (1983). Peer relationships. In P. H. Mussen (Ed.), *Handbook of child psychology* (4th ed.). *Vol. 3: Cognitive development* (pp. 103–196). New York: Wiley.

Howes, C., & Farver, S. A. (1987). Social pretend play in two-year-olds: Effects of age of partner. *Early Childhood Research Quarterly, 2,* 305–314.

Johnson, D. W., Johnson, R. T., Holubec, E. J., & Roy, P. (1984). *Circles of learning: Cooperation in the classroom.* Alexandria, VA: Association for Supervision and Curriculum Development.

Katz, L. G. (1988). Early childhood education: What research tells us. *Phi Delta Kappa Fastback.* Bloomington, IN.

Katz, L. G., & Chard, S. C. (1989). *Engaging children's minds: The project approach.* Norwood, NJ: Ablex.

Katz, L. G., Raths, J. D., & Torres, R. D. (1987). *A place called kindergarten*. Urbana, IL: ERIC Clearinghouse on Elementary and Early Childhood Education.

Kim, S. H. (1990). *The effect of cross age interaction on socially at risk children*. Unpublished doctoral dissertation, University of Illinois, Urbana.

Lew, M., Mesch, D., Johnson, D. W., & Johnson, R. (1986). Positive interdependence, academic and collaborative skills group contingencies, and isolated students. *American Educational Research Journal, 23*, 476–488.

Lippitt, P. (1976). Learning through cross-age helping: Why and how. In V. L. Allen (Ed.), *Children as teachers: Theory and research on tutoring* (pp. 157–168). New York: Academic.

Lougee, M. D. R., & Graziano, W. G. (undated). *Children's relationships with non-agemate peers*. Unpublished manuscript.

Lougee, M. D., Grueneich, R., & Hartup, W. W. (1977). Social interaction in same-age and mixed-age dyads of preschool children. *Child Development, 48*, 1353–1361.

Ludeke, R. J., & Hartup, W. W. (1983). Teaching behavior of 9- and 11-year-old girls in mixed-age and same-age dyads. *Journal of Educational Psychology, 75*, 908–914.

Mize, J., & Ladd, G. W. (in press). Toward the development of successful social skill training for preschool children. In S. F. Asher & J. D. Cole (Eds), *Peer rejection in childhood*. New York: Cambridge University Press.

Mounts, N. S., & Roopnarine, J. L. (1987). Social cognitive play patterns in same-age and mixed-age preschool classrooms. *American Educational Research Journal, 24*, 463–476.

National Association of State Boards of Education. (1988). *Right from the start: The report of the NASBE Task Force on Early Childhood Education*. Alexandria, VA: Author.

Nicholls, J. G. (1979). Quality and equality in intellectual development: The role of motivation in education. *American Psychologist, 34*, 1071–1084.

Papadopoulos, A. (1988). The contact school plan: Visit to the Swedish Contact School (Fajanskolan, Falkenberg). Strasbourg, France: Council of Europe. (ERIC Document Reproduction Service No. ED 292 569)

Parten, M. B. (1933). Social participation among preschool children. *Journal of Abnormal and Social Psychology, 27*, 243–269.

Pratt, D. (1983, April). *Age segregation in schools*. Paper presented at the annual meeting of the American Educational Research Association, Montreal, Quebec, Canada. (ERIC Document Reproduction Service No. ED 231 038)

Radke-Yarrow, M., Zahn-Waxler, C., & Chapman, M. (1983). Children's prosocial dispositions and behavior. In M. Hetherington (Ed.), *Socialization, personality and social development*. In P. H. Mussen (Ed.), *Handbook of child psychology* (Vol. 4). New York: Wiley.

Roopnarine, J. L. (1987). The social individual model: Mixed-age socialization. In J. L. Roopnarine & J. E. Johnson (Eds.), *Approaches to early childhood education* (pp. 143–162). Columbus, OH: Merrill.

Rosenholtz, S. J., & Simpson, C. (1984). Classroom organization and student stratification. *Elementary School Journal, 85*(1), 21–37.

Royal Commission on Education, British Columbia. (1989). *A legacy for learners: Summary of findings (1987–1988)*. British Columbia, Canada: Author.

Russell, T., & Ford, D. F. (1983). Effectiveness of peer tutors versus resource teachers. *Psychology in the Schools, 20,* 436–441.

Shatz, M., & Gelman, R. (1973). The development of communication skills: Modification in the speech of young children as a function of listener. *Monographs of the Society for Research in Child Development, 38*(5, Serial No. 152).

Slavin, R. E. (1987). Developmental and motivational perspectives on cooperative learning: A reconciliation. *Child Development, 58,* 1161–1167.

Stahl, P. C., Stahl, N. A., & Henk, W. A. (undated). *Historical roots, rationales, and applications of peer and cross-age tutoring: A basic primer for practitioners and researchers.* Unpublished paper. (ERIC Document Reproduction Service No. ED 284 660)

Stright, A. L., & French, D. C. (1988). Leadership in mixed-age children's groups. *International Journal of Behavioral Development 11,* 507–515.

Tudge, J. (1986a, May 30). *Beyond conflict: The role of reasoning in collaborative problem solving.* Paper presented at the Piaget Society conference, Philadelphia, PA. (ERIC Document Reproduction Service No. ED 275 395)

Tudge, J. (1986b, April 18). *Collaboration, conflict and cognitive development: The efficacy of joint problem solving.* Paper presented at the Eastern Psychological Association conference, New York. (ERIC Document Reproduction Service No. ED 274 424)

Vygotsky, L. S. (1978). *Mind in society: The development of higher psychological processes.* Edited by M. Cole, V. John-Steiner, S. Scribner, & E. Souberman. Cambridge, MA: Harvard University Press.

Wertsch, J. V. (1985). *Culture, communication, and cognition: Vygotskian perspectives.* Cambridge, England: Cambridge University Press.

Whiting, B. B. (1983). The genesis of prosocial behavior. In D. Bridgeman (Ed.), *The nature of prosocial development* (pp. 221–242). New York: Academic Press.

Whiting, B. B., & Edwards, C. (1988). *Children of different worlds: The formation of social behavior.* Cambridge, MA: Harvard University Press.

Zindell, A. (undated). *A consideration of how cross-age tutoring can improve kindergarten children's skills.* Evanston, IL: National College of Education. (ERIC Document Reproduction Service No. ED 300117)

Appendix

Suggestions for Teachers Implementing Mixed-Age Grouping

P LACING CHILDREN INTO MIXED-AGE GROUPS DOES NOT AUTOMATI-CALLY ASSURE THE REALIZATION OF ALL ITS POTENTIAL BENEFITS. Among the factors to be considered are the staffing patterns and teaching strategies.

Staffing patterns

Ideally, all classes with anywhere from 25 to 35 five- and six-year-olds should have two staff members. For children four years old and younger, the group should be smaller, with at least two adults. If the class is mixed in age (e.g., fours and fives; fives and sixes; fours, fives, and sixes), the group may be somewhat larger than a class of all four-year-olds and should have at least two full-time staff members. The two staff members may work as equal partners or as lead and assistant teachers, depending upon their qualifications and preferences, the group's characteristics, the program, and other considerations.

Teaching strategies

Teaching strategies appropriate for mixed-age groups are the same as for any early childhood setting. However, if all the potential benefits of the mixture are to be maximized and the potential risks minimized, some strategies may deserve special emphasis. They are described briefly below.

Enhancing social development

In a mixed-age class, teachers may have to intervene deliberately to stimulate cross-age interaction, especially at first. In this way, the teacher lets the children know that she expects them to notice and act upon what they learn about each other's concerns. Teachers' appreciation of constructive cross-age interactions will stimulate their occurrence and cultivate a nurturing familylike ethos in the class or center.

1. Suggest that older children assist younger ones and that younger ones request assistance from older ones in social situations.

Aside from helping children become acquainted with each other, the teacher can suggest that older children help younger ones enter group activities and so on and make allowances for younger children's needs. Teachers can encourage younger children to solicit help, advice, attention, directions, and other kinds of assistance from older children in participating in group play and so forth.

2. Encourage older children to assume responsibility for younger ones, and encourage younger ones to rely on older ones.

The teacher may also prompt an older child to assume responsibility for a younger one and, similarly, advise a younger child to depend on an older one for certain kinds of assistance when the situation warrants it. For example, a young child new to the group with little or no experience of other children is often helped to enter it or to feel at home by an older, experienced child's reassurance and advocacy.

Occasionally, a teacher has to tone down excessive zeal on the part of a responsible older child who may take her responsibilities a little too seriously! It takes some children time to learn the distinction between being helpful and being domineering. In such cases the child can be encouraged to supervise in a friendly rather than oppressive manner.

3. Guard against younger childen becoming burdens or nuisances for older ones.

There is often a temptation to exploit older children as helpers and teachers such that their own progress might be impeded. Regular observations and reviews of each individual child's progress and experience in the group will help to minimize this possibility.

4. Help children accept their present limitations.

Mixed-age settings allow younger children to learn what their (temporary) limitations are and how to accept them. They can also learn to anticipate the competences and strengths observed in older classmates. Young children discover that a limitation (due to age, inexperience, etc.) is not a tragedy; some limitations can provide challenges, and others must be accepted gracefully, perhaps only for the moment.

5. Help children develop appreciation of their own earlier efforts and progress.

Teachers can use appropriate opportunities to help older children learn, from their observations of younger ones, about their own progress and how far they have come. Such appreciation of their own less mature behavior may strengthen children's dispositions to be charitable toward the less mature they inevitably encounter. This may, in turn, reduce the negative effects of some teachers' tendencies to praise a child repeatedly for being a "big boy" or "big girl" and to intimidate children by indicating that their undesirable behavior is not fitting for the class they are in, but rather for the one from which they have been promoted.

6. Discourage stereotyping by age.

If older children exhibit a tendency to disparage the efforts of younger ones by calling them "dummies" or "cry babies," the teacher should discourage them from doing so and teach them instead how to be helpful and appreciative of younger ones' efforts. Occasional gentle and friendly reminders of their own earlier behavior can also strengthen acceptance of others' efforts. For example, if two children are sent to convey a message to the center director or school principal, it should not always be the older one who carries it. He might simply observe and make sure that the task is carried out properly while the younger child actually makes the request or gives the explanation.

Enhancing emotional development

There is abundant evidence that children respond to the feelings and moods of those around them very early in life (see Radke-Yarrow, Zahn-Waxler, & Chapman, 1983). Teachers can channel this responsiveness in at least two ways:

1. Alert children to their peers' needs, feelings, and desires.

The teacher can help children's emotional development by *interpreting* children's feelings, wishes, and desires to each other. The teacher explains or describes to one child or a group the feelings, wishes, or desires she believes another child has in a matter-of-fact way, conveying information and insight clearly and respectfully.

2. Encourage children to give and to accept comfort from each other at times of special stress, separation anxiety, and so forth.

The teacher can arouse sympathy by suggesting to one child that she probably knows what it feels like to miss someone or to experience sad times. The teacher should say this without attributing thoughtlessness to the child in question and without sentimentality.

Encouraging intellectual development

When the curriculum encourages children to work together on a wide variety of tasks, projects, and other activities, the teacher can use cross-age interaction to promote a range of intellectual and cognitive benefits.

1. Alert children to their peers' interests.

This occurs when teachers refer children to one another. For example, if a child reports with great enthusiasm some interest or event in her life, the teacher can remind her that another child is also interested in the same thing and might want to hear about it. Similarly, in discussion with small groups of children, the teacher might ask one child to respond to what another has said, simply by asking something like, "What do you think about that, Annie?" Or, she can ask the group, "Have you any suggestions for Jerome's project on lizards?" Such strategies indicate to the children that the lines of communication can go from child to child as well as from child to teacher and teacher to child.

2. Alert children to their peers' skills as appropriate.

When one child asks for help with writing something on his painting or feeding the class rabbit, the teacher can recommend a particular classmate to ask because she can write well or can probably show the requester how to do the chore. Occasionally, such suggestions fail: Sometimes the requester insists that he wants the teacher's help and not another child's, and occasionally the recommended helper is too busy or for some reason unwilling to help. In the first case, the teacher has to use her judgment in deciding whether to insist on her first suggestion or to accede to the child's demand. In the second case, it is important to respect the other child's wishes and to explain to the requester that as the other is busy at the moment, he must either wait awhile or try an alternative approach.

Part of project work includes making books about what has been done, what has been learned, and so forth (see Katz & Chard, 1989). Some of the older, more experienced children get tired of doing the illustrations and coloring the pictures. Therefore, the younger children can do these tasks while the older ones write and bind the book. Similarly, if a group decides to make labels, graphs, or pictures of something related to their work, the older children could be encouraged to do the labeling and to take dictations from the others, while the younger children continue with less demanding but equally important aspects of the collaborative effort. Those who can write or spell can take responsibility for helping those who cannot yet do so. These kinds of activities are similar to those that Clay (1979) refers to as socially guided literacy.

3. Encourage children to read to others and to listen to others read.

The reading that one child does for another may be no more than storytelling on the basis of the pictures in the book, but it cannot fail to encourage the child to see reading to another as important. Furthermore, the appreciation — if not admiration — expressed by the younger listener may strengthen the "reader's" motivation to progress with learning to read.

4. Help older children think through appropriate roles for younger ones.

Imagine that a group of children are working on a play, for example, and the producers dismiss the youngest members of the class as lacking sufficient or pertinent abilities to participate in it. The teacher can help by encouraging the director to think of simple easy roles or by pointing out special abilities of the younger children that she is aware of.

While these practices are especially useful in mixed-age and mixed-ability groups, they can be adapted for use in any class. They also tend to reduce the children's dependency on the teacher.

Information About NAEYC

NAEYC is ...

... a membership-supported organization of people committed to fostering the growth and development of children from birth through age eight. Membership is open to all who share a desire to serve and act on behalf of the needs and rights of young children.

NAEYC provides ...

... educational services and resources to adults who work with and for children, including

• *Young Children, the* journal for early childhood educators

• **Books, posters, brochures,** and **videos** to expand your knowledge and commitment to young children, with topics including infants, curriculum, research, discipline, teacher education, and parent involvement

• An **Annual Conference** that brings people from all over the country to share their expertise and advocate on behalf of children and families

• **Week of the Young Child** celebrations sponsored by NAEYC Affiliate Groups across the nation to call public attention to the needs and rights of children and families

• **Insurance plans** for individuals and programs

• **Public affairs** information for knowledgeable advocacy efforts at all levels of government and through the media

• The **National Academy of Early Childhood Programs,** a voluntary accreditation system for high-quality programs for children

• The **National Institute for Early Childhood Professional Development,** providing resources and services to improve professional preparation and development of early childhood educators

• The **Information Service,** a centralized source of information sharing, distribution, and collaboration

For free information about membership, publications, or other NAEYC services ...

• call NAEYC at 202–232–8777 or 800–424–2460

• or write to the National Association for the Education of Young Children, 1509 16th Street, N.W., Washington, DC 20036–1426.